Copyright © 2021 Pizza Cat
All rights reserved.
ISBN-13: 9798470453921

THIS BOOK IS DEDICATED TO...

...ANYONE WHO HAS EVER HAD TO
EAT THEIR LUNCH ON A JUMPSEAT,
NEXT TO A LAVATORY.

Check out other Pizza Cat books:
Amazon.com/Author/PizzaCat

If you **love** this book, don't forget to rate us on **Amazon**.

☆☆☆☆☆

If you've got **suggestions**, we'd **love** to hear from you:
PizzaCatBooks@gmail.com

THIS BOOK BELONGS TO:

_____
NAME & BASE

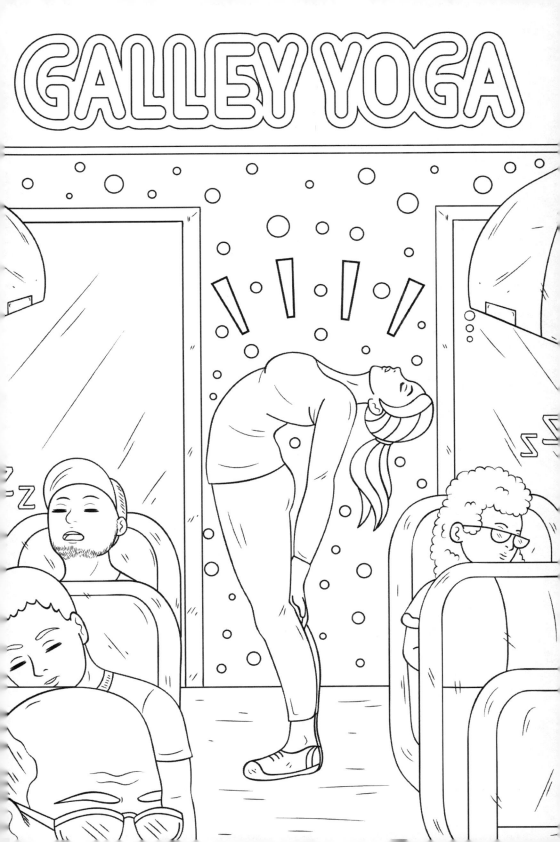

HOTEL ROOM PRE-CHECK

CREW SCHEDULING MELTDOWN

A MILE OF HIGHWAY WILL ONLY TAKE YOU A MILE. A MILE OF RUNWAY WILL TAKE YOU *anywhere!*

ABOUT THE AUTHOR

Pizza Cat was born into a litter of 8 other slices of pizza kittens. With her purrrfect toppings, she clawed her way to the top of the pizza box to bring forth her uniqueness to the world. Right meow, more than ever, she hopes to bring a bit of joy to everyone who purrrchases her cheesy creations. Thank you! ♥

Don't forget to **rate this book on Amazon** if you've enjoyed it!

☆☆☆☆☆

Check out other Pizza Cat books:
Amazon.com/Author/PizzaCat

Made in the USA
Columbia, SC
11 July 2023